ETHEREUM INVESTMENT STRATEGY

Profitable Trading Strategies for Ethereum Investors

REBELLO M. POSTON

Copyright

All rights reserved. No part of this publication may be reproduced, distributed, or transmitted in any form or by any means, including photocopying, recording, or other electronic or mechanical methods, without the prior written permission of the publisher, except in the case of brief quotations embodied in critical reviews and certain other noncommercial uses permitted by copyright law.

Copyright© Rebello M. Poston, 2024.

TABLE OF CONTENTS

INTRODUCTION

CHAPTER 1: INTRODUCTION TO ETHEREUM AND BLOCKCHAIN TECHNOLOGY
- Understanding Blockchain Fundamentals
- The Evolution of Ethereum
- Key Differences Between Bitcoin and Ethereum
- The Role of Smart Contracts

CHAPTER 2: SETTING UP FOR ETHEREUM INVESTMENT
- Creating a Digital Wallet
- Selecting a Reliable Exchange
- Security Best Practices
- Regulatory Considerations

CHAPTER 3: MARKET ANALYSIS AND RESEARCH
- Fundamental Analysis of Ethereum
- Technical Analysis Techniques
- Understanding Market Sentiment
- Key Metrics and Indicators for Ethereum

CHAPTER 4: DEVELOPING AN INVESTMENT STRATEGY
- Risk Assessment and Management
- Diversification Techniques
- Short-term vs Long-term Investment

Strategies
　　- Identifying Entry and Exit Points

CHAPTER 5: ADVANCED INVESTMENT TACTICS
　　- Leveraging Decentralized Finance (DeFi)
　　- Yield Farming and Staking
　　- Utilizing Ethereum Derivatives
　　- Navigating Market Volatility

CHAPTER 6: MONITORING AND ADJUSTING YOUR PORTFOLIO
　　- Performance Tracking Tools
　　- Rebalancing Your Portfolio
　　- Adapting to Market Changes
　　- Learning from Investment Mistakes

CONCLUSION

INTRODUCTION

"Ethereum Investment Strategy," a comprehensive guide designed to help you navigate the dynamic and often complex world of Ethereum investments. Whether you are a seasoned investor looking to diversify your portfolio or a newcomer eager to explore the potential of blockchain technology, this book aims to equip you with the knowledge and tools needed to make informed investment decisions.

Ethereum, launched in 2015 by Vitalik Buterin and his team, has rapidly emerged as one of the most influential platforms in the cryptocurrency space. Unlike Bitcoin, which primarily functions as digital gold, Ethereum offers a versatile ecosystem that supports smart contracts and decentralized applications (dApps). This flexibility has positioned Ethereum at the forefront of the blockchain revolution, fostering innovation in areas such as finance, supply chain management, and digital identity.

Investing in Ethereum presents unique opportunities but also comes with its own set of challenges. The market is known for its volatility, and the technology itself is continually evolving. Understanding the fundamentals of Ethereum and the broader blockchain landscape is crucial for developing a sound investment strategy.

In this book, we will begin with the basics, exploring the core concepts of blockchain technology and the distinctive features of Ethereum. You will learn how to set up a digital wallet, select a reliable exchange, and implement security measures to protect your assets. We will delve into market analysis techniques, helping you understand both fundamental and technical aspects of Ethereum investing.

As you progress, you will discover various investment strategies tailored to different risk profiles and investment goals. From short-term trading to long-term holding, and from leveraging decentralized finance (DeFi) opportunities to advanced tactics like yield farming and staking, this book covers a wide array of methods to enhance your investment portfolio.

Finally, we will discuss how to monitor and adjust your investments in response to market changes, ensuring that your strategy remains aligned with your financial objectives. By the end of this journey, you will be well-prepared to navigate the Ethereum investment landscape with confidence and foresight.

CHAPTER 1: INTRODUCTION TO ETHEREUM AND BLOCKCHAIN TECHNOLOGY

UNDERSTANDING BLOCKCHAIN FUNDAMENTALS

Blockchain technology serves as the foundation for cryptocurrencies like Ethereum, revolutionizing traditional systems of record-keeping and transaction processing. At its core, a blockchain is a decentralized, distributed ledger that records transactions across a network of computers in a secure and immutable manner.

1. Decentralization: Unlike centralized systems where a single authority controls the database, blockchain operates on a decentralized network of nodes. Each node stores a copy of the entire blockchain, ensuring transparency and eliminating the need for a central authority.

2. Distributed Ledger: Every transaction on the blockchain is recorded as a block, which contains a timestamp and a cryptographic hash of the previous block, creating a chronological chain of blocks. This distributed ledger provides a transparent and tamper-resistant record of all transactions.

3. Consensus Mechanisms: To validate and add new transactions to the blockchain, consensus mechanisms are employed. These mechanisms ensure that all nodes in the network agree on the validity of transactions without the need for a trusted intermediary. Proof of Work (PoW) and Proof of Stake (PoS) are two common consensus algorithms.

4. Immutability: Once a transaction is recorded on the blockchain and confirmed by the network, it cannot be altered or deleted. This immutability feature ensures the integrity of the data stored on the blockchain, making it resistant to fraud and manipulation.

5. Smart Contracts: Ethereum introduced the concept of smart contracts, self-executing contracts with the terms of the agreement directly written into code. Smart contracts automate and enforce the execution of transactions when predefined conditions are met, enabling a wide range of decentralized applications (dApps) to be built on the Ethereum platform.

Understanding these fundamental principles of blockchain technology lays the groundwork for comprehending the capabilities and implications of Ethereum and other blockchain-based systems. As we delve deeper into Ethereum investment strategy, this knowledge will serve as a valuable guide in navigating the evolving landscape of decentralized finance and digital assets.

THE EVOLUTION OF ETHEREUM

Since its inception in 2015, Ethereum has undergone significant evolution, transforming from a pioneering blockchain project to a global platform for decentralized applications (dApps), smart contracts, and digital assets. Understanding the key milestones in Ethereum's development provides valuable insight into its growth trajectory and the broader blockchain ecosystem.

1. Genesis: Birth of Ethereum: Ethereum was conceptualized by Vitalik Buterin in late 2013 and officially launched on July 30, 2015. The Ethereum blockchain introduced the revolutionary concept of smart contracts, enabling developers to create programmable agreements that execute automatically when predefined conditions are met. This innovation laid the groundwork for a wide range of decentralized applications.

2. Homestead Release: In March 2016, Ethereum underwent its first major upgrade with the release of Homestead. This upgrade brought improvements to the Ethereum Virtual Machine (EVM), making it more secure and efficient. Homestead marked Ethereum's transition from a beta phase to a stable and reliable platform for developers and users alike.

3. The Rise of Decentralized Finance (DeFi): One of the most significant developments on the Ethereum platform has been the emergence of decentralized finance (DeFi) applications. DeFi protocols enable users to access a wide range of financial services, including lending, borrowing, trading, and earning interest, without relying on traditional financial intermediaries. The explosive growth of DeFi has positioned Ethereum as the leading platform for decentralized finance innovation.

4. Ethereum 2.0: The Transition to Proof of Stake: Ethereum 2.0, also known as Eth2 or Serenity, represents a major upgrade to the Ethereum network aimed at improving scalability, security, and sustainability. The most significant change in Ethereum 2.0 is the transition from the energy-intensive Proof of Work (PoW) consensus mechanism to the more environmentally friendly Proof of Stake (PoS) mechanism. This transition will enhance the network's efficiency and enable it to process a significantly higher number of transactions.

5. Continued Innovation and Adoption: Ethereum continues to evolve rapidly, with ongoing upgrades and innovations driving its growth and adoption. From the integration of layer 2 scaling solutions to the expansion of interoperability with other blockchain networks, Ethereum remains at the forefront of blockchain technology development.

The evolution of Ethereum reflects the relentless pursuit of innovation and the commitment to building a decentralized, open-source platform that empowers individuals and organizations worldwide. As Ethereum continues to evolve, it will play a pivotal role in shaping the future of finance, technology, and beyond.

KEY DIFFERENCES BETWEEN BITCOIN AND ETHEREUM

Bitcoin and Ethereum are two of the most prominent cryptocurrencies, each with its own unique features and use cases. While they share some similarities as blockchain-based digital assets, there are several key differences that set them apart.

1. Purpose and Functionality:

   - **Bitcoin (BTC):** Bitcoin was created as a decentralized digital currency and store of value. Its primary purpose is to facilitate peer-to-peer transactions and serve as a hedge against traditional fiat currencies and inflation.

   - **Ethereum (ETH):** Ethereum, on the other hand, is a decentralized platform that enables developers to build and deploy smart contracts and decentralized applications (dApps). While Ethereum can be used as a digital currency (Ether), its main function is to provide a platform for executing programmable agreements and decentralized applications.

2. Smart Contracts and dApps:

   - **Bitcoin:** Bitcoin's scripting language is relatively simple and limited, primarily designed for transferring value between addresses. It does not support the creation of complex smart contracts or decentralized applications.

- **Ethereum:** Ethereum introduced the concept of smart contracts, which are self-executing contracts with the terms of the agreement directly written into code. This capability enables developers to create a wide range of decentralized applications, spanning industries such as finance, gaming, and supply chain management.

3. Consensus Mechanism:

- **Bitcoin:** Bitcoin operates on a Proof of Work (PoW) consensus mechanism, where miners compete to solve cryptographic puzzles to validate transactions and secure the network.

- **Ethereum:** While Ethereum currently operates on a PoW mechanism similar to Bitcoin, it is in the process of transitioning to a more energy-efficient Proof of Stake (PoS) mechanism with Ethereum 2.0. PoS relies on validators who hold and stake Ether to secure the network, rather than miners competing for block rewards.

4. Supply Cap:

- **Bitcoin:** Bitcoin has a fixed supply cap of 21 million coins, making it a deflationary asset. This scarcity is built into the protocol and is one of the key features driving its value as a store of value.

- **Ethereum:** Ethereum does not have a fixed supply cap, and new Ether tokens are issued as block rewards to miners. However, there are ongoing discussions within the Ethereum community about implementing Ethereum Improvement Proposals (EIPs) to potentially cap the total supply of Ether in the future.

While both Bitcoin and Ethereum are significant players in the cryptocurrency space, their distinct features and use cases cater to different needs and objectives within the blockchain ecosystem. Understanding these key differences is essential for investors and developers seeking to leverage the unique capabilities of each platform.

THE ROLE OF SMART CONTRACTS

Smart contracts represent a revolutionary concept introduced by Ethereum, enabling programmable agreements to be executed automatically without the need for intermediaries. These self-executing contracts are written in code and reside on the blockchain, offering a wide range of applications across various industries. Understanding the role of smart contracts is essential for grasping the transformative potential of blockchain technology.

1. **Automation of Transactions:** Smart contracts automate the execution of transactions based on predefined conditions. Once deployed on the blockchain, smart contracts autonomously enforce the terms of the agreement without the need for human intervention. This automation streamlines processes, reduces costs, and eliminates the risk of fraud or manipulation associated with traditional contracts.

2. **Trustless Interactions:** Smart contracts operate in a trustless environment, meaning that parties can transact with each other directly without relying on intermediaries or third-party trust. The code of the smart contract serves as the ultimate authority, ensuring transparency and immutability of the agreement. This trustless nature enhances

security and eliminates the need for costly and time-consuming legal procedures.

3. Decentralized Applications (dApps): Smart contracts serve as the backbone of decentralized applications (dApps) built on the Ethereum platform. These dApps leverage smart contracts to automate various functions, such as financial transactions, asset management, identity verification, and supply chain tracking. By eliminating centralized control and intermediaries, dApps promote transparency, censorship resistance, and user sovereignty.

4. Conditional Payments and Escrow Services: Smart contracts enable conditional payments, where funds are released only when predefined conditions are met. This feature is particularly useful for escrow services, where a neutral party holds funds until both parties fulfill their obligations. Smart contracts ensure that funds are released fairly and automatically based on the agreed-upon conditions, reducing the risk of disputes and fraud.

5. Tokenization and Asset Management: Smart contracts facilitate the tokenization of assets, representing real-world assets as digital tokens on the blockchain. These tokens can represent ownership rights to physical assets such as real estate, art, or commodities, allowing for fractional ownership, liquidity, and efficient asset management. Smart contracts automate the transfer and management of these digital assets, enabling seamless peer-to-peer transactions.

Smart contracts play a pivotal role in unlocking the full potential of blockchain technology by automating transactions, enabling trustless interactions, powering decentralized applications, facilitating conditional payments, and tokenizing assets. As the adoption of blockchain technology continues to expand, smart contracts will remain a cornerstone of innovation, driving efficiency, transparency, and security across diverse industries.

CHAPTER 2: SETTING UP FOR ETHEREUM INVESTMENT

CREATING A DIGITAL WALLET

Creating a digital wallet is the first step towards engaging with cryptocurrencies like Ethereum. A digital wallet, also known as a cryptocurrency wallet, is a software program or hardware device that enables users to securely store, send, and receive digital currencies. Here's a guide on how to create a digital wallet for Ethereum:

1. Choose a Wallet Type: There are several types of digital wallets available, including software wallets (desktop, mobile, or web-based) and hardware wallets (physical devices). Consider your preferences for convenience, security, and accessibility when selecting a wallet type.

2. Select a Software Wallet: If you prefer a software wallet, you can choose from a variety of options available for Ethereum, such as MetaMask, MyEtherWallet (MEW), Trust Wallet, or Coinbase Wallet. These wallets offer user-friendly interfaces and can be accessed from desktop computers, mobile devices, or web browsers.

3. Download and Install the Wallet: Visit the official website or app store of your chosen wallet provider and download the wallet application to your device. Follow the instructions to install the wallet software and create a new wallet account.

4. Secure Your Wallet: After installing the wallet, you will typically be prompted to set up a strong password or passphrase to secure your wallet. Make sure to choose a unique and complex password and consider enabling additional security features such as two-factor authentication (2FA) for added protection.

5. Backup Your Wallet: Most wallets will provide you with a recovery phrase or seed phrase, which is a series of words that can be used to restore access to your wallet in case you forget your password or lose your device. Write down this recovery phrase and store it in a safe and secure location, preferably offline.

6. Receive and Send Ethereum: Once your wallet is set up and secured, you can generate an Ethereum address, which serves as your unique identifier on the blockchain. You can share this address with others to receive Ethereum into your wallet. To send Ethereum, simply enter the recipient's address and the amount you wish to send, and authorize the transaction using your wallet's interface.

7. Stay Informed: Keep your wallet software up to date with the latest security patches and updates released by the wallet provider. Stay informed about best practices for securely storing and managing your digital assets, and be cautious of phishing attempts or scams targeting cryptocurrency users.

By following these steps, you can create a digital wallet for Ethereum and begin securely storing, sending, and receiving Ether and other ERC-20 tokens. Always prioritize security and diligence when managing your digital assets to protect against potential risks and ensure a positive experience with cryptocurrency ownership.

SELECTING A RELIABLE EXCHANGE

Choosing a reliable cryptocurrency exchange is crucial for safely buying, selling, and trading Ethereum and other digital assets. With numerous exchanges available, it's essential to consider factors such as security, fees, liquidity, user experience, and regulatory compliance when making your selection. Here's a guide on how to select a reliable exchange for Ethereum:

1. Security Measures: Ensure that the exchange prioritizes security measures to protect users' funds and personal information. Look for features such as two-factor authentication (2FA), cold storage for storing a significant portion of funds offline, encryption protocols, and regular security audits.

2. Reputation and Trustworthiness: Research the reputation and track record of the exchange within the cryptocurrency community. Check online reviews, user feedback, and social media channels to gauge the exchange's reliability, transparency, and responsiveness to customer inquiries or issues.

3. Regulatory Compliance: Choose an exchange that complies with relevant regulatory requirements in your jurisdiction. Look for exchanges that adhere to Know Your Customer

(KYC) and Anti-Money Laundering (AML) regulations, as these measures help enhance security and mitigate the risk of illicit activities.

4. Liquidity and Trading Volume: Opt for an exchange with high liquidity and trading volume for Ethereum and other cryptocurrencies. Higher liquidity ensures tighter bid-ask spreads and faster execution of trades, reducing the risk of slippage and enabling you to enter and exit positions more efficiently.

5. Supported Trading Pairs: Check whether the exchange supports the trading pairs you intend to trade, such as ETH/USD, ETH/BTC, or ETH/USDT. A diverse selection of trading pairs provides flexibility and opportunities for portfolio diversification.

6. User Interface and Experience: Evaluate the exchange's user interface and experience to ensure it is intuitive, responsive, and easy to navigate. Look for features such as advanced charting tools, order types, and customizable trading dashboards to enhance your trading experience.

7. Fees and Costs: Compare the fee structure of different exchanges, including trading fees, deposit and withdrawal fees, and any other applicable charges. Consider factors such as maker and taker fees, volume-based fee discounts, and fiat currency deposit/withdrawal fees when assessing the overall cost of trading on the exchange.

8. Customer Support: Choose an exchange that offers responsive and reliable customer support to address any issues or inquiries promptly. Look for exchanges that provide multiple channels of communication, such as live chat, email support, and a comprehensive knowledge base or FAQ section.

By carefully evaluating these factors and conducting thorough research, you can select a reliable cryptocurrency exchange that meets your trading needs and provides a secure and seamless experience for buying, selling, and trading Ethereum and other digital assets. Always exercise caution and due diligence when dealing with exchanges, and consider starting with smaller transactions until you become familiar with the platform's features and functionality.

SECURITY BEST PRACTICES

Implementing robust security measures is essential when dealing with cryptocurrencies like Ethereum to safeguard your funds and personal information from potential threats. Here are some security best practices to follow:

1. Use a Secure Wallet: Choose a reputable and secure wallet for storing your Ethereum, such as a hardware wallet (e.g., Ledger Nano S, Trezor) or a software wallet (e.g., MetaMask, MyEtherWallet). Hardware wallets offer enhanced security by keeping your private keys offline, while software wallets provide convenience for everyday transactions.

2. Secure Your Private Keys: Keep your private keys and recovery phrases offline and in a safe place, such as a hardware wallet or a physical paper wallet. Never share your private keys or recovery phrases with anyone, and avoid storing them digitally where they could be vulnerable to hacking or theft.

3. Enable Two-Factor Authentication (2FA): Enable two-factor authentication (2FA) on your cryptocurrency exchange accounts and wallet applications to add an extra layer of security. Use authenticator apps like Google Authenticator or hardware tokens for 2FA instead of relying solely on SMS-based authentication, which can be susceptible to SIM swapping attacks.

4. Be Cautious of Phishing Attempts: Beware of phishing attempts and fraudulent websites that mimic legitimate cryptocurrency exchanges, wallets, or ICOs. Always double-check URLs, verify the authenticity of websites, and never enter your login credentials or private keys on unfamiliar or suspicious websites.

5. Keep Software Up to Date: Regularly update your wallet software, operating system, antivirus software, and other security tools to patch vulnerabilities and protect against malware, viruses, and other cyber threats. Enable automatic updates whenever possible to ensure you have the latest security patches installed.

6. Use Secure Networks: Avoid accessing your cryptocurrency accounts or conducting transactions over public Wi-Fi networks or unsecured internet connections, as they can be prone to interception and hacking. Use a secure and private internet connection, such as a trusted home network or a virtual private network (VPN), when accessing sensitive financial information.

7. Diversify Your Holdings: Diversify your cryptocurrency holdings across multiple wallets and exchanges to mitigate the risk of a single point of failure. Consider spreading your investments across different asset classes and cryptocurrencies to reduce exposure to market volatility and potential security breaches.

8. Exercise Caution with Third-Party Services: Be cautious when using third-party services such as cryptocurrency lending platforms, staking pools, or decentralized finance (DeFi) protocols. Thoroughly research the reputation, security practices, and terms of service of these services before entrusting them with your funds.

Following these security best practices and remaining vigilant against potential threats, you can enhance the safety and integrity of your Ethereum holdings and protect yourself from unauthorized access, fraud, and theft in the ever-evolving landscape of cryptocurrency.

REGULATORY CONSIDERATIONS

Navigating regulatory considerations is essential when engaging with cryptocurrencies like Ethereum to ensure compliance with applicable laws and regulations. Here are some key regulatory considerations to keep in mind:

1. Know Your Jurisdiction: Understand the regulatory environment for cryptocurrencies and blockchain technology in your jurisdiction, as regulations vary significantly from country to country. Stay informed about any updates or changes to regulatory frameworks, including tax laws, licensing requirements, and reporting obligations.

2. Compliance with AML/KYC Regulations: Many jurisdictions require cryptocurrency exchanges, wallets, and other service providers to implement Anti-Money Laundering (AML) and Know Your Customer (KYC) measures to prevent illicit activities such as money laundering, terrorist financing, and fraud. Ensure that you comply with these regulations when using cryptocurrency services.

3. Tax Obligations: Cryptocurrency transactions may have tax implications depending on your jurisdiction's tax laws. Familiarize yourself with the tax treatment of cryptocurrencies, including capital gains taxes, income taxes, and reporting requirements for buying, selling, trading, and holding cryptocurrencies like Ethereum.

4. Regulatory Compliance for Businesses: If you operate a business that deals with cryptocurrencies, such as an exchange, wallet service, or ICO/STO platform, ensure that you comply with relevant regulatory requirements, licensing obligations, and consumer protection laws. Seek legal counsel to navigate complex regulatory landscapes and mitigate legal risks.

5. Securities Regulations: Tokens issued through Initial Coin Offerings (ICOs) or Security Token Offerings (STOs) may be subject to securities regulations in certain jurisdictions. Determine whether your token falls under securities laws and comply with registration, disclosure, and investor protection requirements to avoid regulatory scrutiny and legal consequences.

6. Stay Informed and Engage with Regulators: Stay updated on regulatory developments and engage with regulators, policymakers, industry associations, and legal experts to understand the evolving regulatory landscape and advocate for clear, fair, and innovation-friendly regulations. Participate in public consultations, industry conferences, and regulatory discussions to contribute to the shaping of regulatory frameworks.

7. Implement Compliance Measures: Implement robust compliance measures and risk management practices within your organization to ensure adherence to regulatory requirements and mitigate legal and reputational risks. Develop internal policies and procedures for AML/KYC compliance, customer due diligence, transaction monitoring, and reporting suspicious activities.

By proactively addressing regulatory considerations and adopting a compliance-first approach, you can navigate the regulatory landscape effectively, build trust with regulators and stakeholders, and contribute to the long-term sustainability and legitimacy of the cryptocurrency ecosystem, including Ethereum.

CHAPTER 3: MARKET ANALYSIS AND RESEARCH

FUNDAMENTAL ANALYSIS OF ETHEREUM
Fundamental analysis of Ethereum involves evaluating the underlying factors that influence its value, adoption, and long-term prospects. Here's a guide on conducting fundamental analysis for Ethereum:

1. Technology and Development: Assess Ethereum's technology stack, including its scalability, security, and usability. Stay informed about ongoing development efforts, protocol upgrades, and improvements such as Ethereum 2.0, which aims to transition the network to a more scalable and sustainable infrastructure.

2. Use Cases and Adoption: Evaluate Ethereum's use cases and adoption across various industries and applications, such as decentralized finance (DeFi), non-fungible tokens (NFTs), decentralized applications (dApps), supply chain management, and identity verification. Monitor adoption metrics, network activity, and transaction volume to gauge Ethereum's utility and demand.

3. Developer Activity and Ecosystem Growth: Monitor developer activity, community engagement, and ecosystem growth within the Ethereum community. Track metrics such as the number of active developers, GitHub commits, and the size and diversity of the dApp ecosystem to assess Ethereum's vibrancy and innovation potential.

4. Network Security and Decentralization: Evaluate Ethereum's network security and decentralization properties, including the distribution of nodes, mining pools, and staking validators. Assess the level of network participation, hash rate distribution, and security features such as Ethereum's proof-of-work (PoW) and upcoming proof-of-stake (PoS) consensus mechanisms.

5. Market Sentiment and Investor Confidence: Monitor market sentiment and investor confidence in Ethereum, as reflected in price trends, trading volumes, social media activity, and sentiment analysis tools. Pay attention to macroeconomic factors, regulatory developments, and geopolitical events that may impact Ethereum's price dynamics and market sentiment.

6. Competitive Landscape: Analyze Ethereum's competitive position relative to other blockchain platforms and cryptocurrencies, including Bitcoin, alternative smart contract platforms (e.g., Binance Smart Chain, Solana), and emerging technologies (e.g., Polkadot, Cardano). Consider Ethereum's strengths, weaknesses, opportunities, and threats in comparison to its peers.

7. Long-Term Value Proposition: Formulate a long-term outlook for Ethereum based on its fundamental strengths, adoption trajectory, technological innovations, and ecosystem growth potential. Consider factors such as network effects, first-mover advantage, network effects, and Ethereum's role in shaping the future of decentralized finance, digital assets, and Web3.

Conducting fundamental analysis of Ethereum, investors can gain insights into its intrinsic value, growth prospects, and investment potential. However, it's essential to complement fundamental analysis with technical analysis, market sentiment analysis, and risk management strategies to make well-informed investment decisions in the dynamic and evolving cryptocurrency market.

TECHNICAL ANALYSIS TECHNIQUES

Technical analysis involves analyzing historical price data and market statistics to forecast future price movements and identify trading opportunities. Here are some popular technical analysis techniques used by traders in the cryptocurrency market, including Ethereum:

1. Candlestick Patterns: Candlestick patterns, such as bullish engulfing, bearish engulfing, doji, hammer, and shooting star, provide visual cues about market sentiment and potential trend reversals. Traders use candlestick patterns to identify entry and exit points and assess market psychology.

2. Support and Resistance Levels: Support and resistance levels are price levels where buying or selling pressure tends to converge, resulting in potential reversals or continuation of trends. Traders use support and resistance levels to identify key price levels for placing stop-loss orders, setting profit targets, and managing risk.

3. Moving Averages: Moving averages, such as the simple moving average (SMA) and exponential moving average (EMA), smooth out price data to identify trends and momentum. Traders use moving averages to assess the direction of the trend, identify trend reversals, and generate buy or sell signals based on crossover patterns.

4. Relative Strength Index (RSI): The Relative Strength Index (RSI) is a momentum oscillator that measures the speed and change of price movements. Traders use the RSI to identify overbought and oversold conditions, divergence patterns, and potential trend reversals. A reading above 70 indicates overbought conditions, while a reading below 30 indicates oversold conditions.

5. Fibonacci Retracement Levels: Fibonacci retracement levels, such as 23.6%, 38.2%, 50%, 61.8%, and 78.6%, are key support and resistance levels based on Fibonacci ratios. Traders use Fibonacci retracement levels to identify potential reversal points or price targets during market corrections or trend pullbacks.

6. Volume Analysis: Volume analysis involves analyzing trading volume to confirm price trends, identify accumulation or distribution patterns, and assess the strength of market movements. Traders use volume analysis to validate trend signals and detect potential trend reversals based on volume spikes or divergences.

7. Trendlines and Chart Patterns: Trendlines and chart patterns, such as triangles, flags, pennants, and head and shoulders patterns, help traders identify trend continuation or reversal patterns. Traders use trendlines and chart patterns to visualize price trends, project price targets, and plan trading strategies based on breakout or breakdown signals.

8. Ichimoku Cloud: The Ichimoku Cloud indicator provides a comprehensive overview of price action, trend direction, support and resistance levels, and momentum. Traders use the Ichimoku Cloud to identify trend reversals, assess market sentiment, and generate buy or sell signals based on cloud crossovers and other components of the indicator.

Incorporating these technical analysis techniques into their trading strategies, traders can gain insights into market dynamics, improve their timing of trades, and make more informed decisions when trading Ethereum and other cryptocurrencies. However, it's essential to combine technical analysis with fundamental analysis and risk management principles to develop a well-rounded trading approach.

UNDERSTANDING MARKET SENTIMENT

Understanding market sentiment is crucial for traders and investors to gauge the overall mood and attitude of market participants towards Ethereum and other cryptocurrencies. Here's how to interpret and analyze market sentiment:

1. Sentiment Indicators: Sentiment indicators, such as social media sentiment, sentiment analysis tools, and surveys, provide insights into the prevailing sentiment among cryptocurrency traders and investors. Analyze sentiment indicators to identify bullish or bearish sentiment trends and potential shifts in market sentiment.

2. Fear and Greed Index: The Fear and Greed Index measures the level of fear and greed in the cryptocurrency market based on various factors, such as price volatility, trading volume, and investor behavior. A high Fear and Greed Index reading indicates greed and potential overbought conditions, while a low reading indicates fear and potential oversold conditions.

3. Crypto News and Media Coverage: Monitor cryptocurrency news websites, forums, social media platforms, and mainstream media outlets for news articles, opinion pieces, and discussions about Ethereum. Pay attention to significant news events, regulatory developments, technological advancements, and market analysis to gauge market sentiment and investor sentiment.

4. Market Sentiment Analysis Tools: Use sentiment analysis tools and sentiment aggregators to analyze sentiment data from various sources and platforms, such as Twitter, Reddit, Telegram, and online forums. These tools use natural language processing (NLP) algorithms to analyze text data and quantify sentiment indicators, such as positive, negative, or neutral sentiment.

5. Price Action and Technical Analysis: Analyze price action, trading volume, and technical indicators to interpret market sentiment from a technical perspective. Look for patterns, trends, and momentum signals that reflect bullish or bearish sentiment, such as trend reversals, chart patterns, and divergences between price and indicators.

6. Contrarian Investing: Consider contrarian investing strategies based on market sentiment extremes and sentiment reversals. Contrarian investors buy when sentiment is excessively bearish and sell when sentiment is excessively bullish, taking advantage of market sentiment swings and potential mean reversion.

7. Sentimental Analysis of Market Participants: Understand the psychology and behavior of different market participants, such as retail traders, institutional investors, whales, and market makers. Analyze their actions, sentiment, and positioning in the market to assess their influence on Ethereum's price dynamics and overall market sentiment.

Combining these approaches, traders and investors can gain valuable insights into market sentiment, sentiment trends, and sentiment shifts in the cryptocurrency market. However, it's essential to consider multiple factors, conduct thorough analysis, and exercise caution when interpreting market sentiment to make well-informed trading and investment decisions in the dynamic and often volatile cryptocurrency market.

KEY METRICS AND INDICATORS FOR ETHEREUM

Key metrics and indicators provide valuable insights into the performance, adoption, and health of the Ethereum network. Here are some essential metrics and indicators to monitor when analyzing Ethereum:

1. Price: Ethereum's price is a fundamental metric that reflects market demand, investor sentiment, and overall market conditions. Monitor Ethereum's price in various fiat currencies and compare it to historical price data to identify trends and potential trading opportunities.

2. Market Capitalization: Ethereum's market capitalization represents the total value of all Ethereum tokens in circulation and is calculated by multiplying the current price by the total supply. Market capitalization provides a measure of Ethereum's overall value and ranking relative to other cryptocurrencies.

3. Network Hash Rate: Ethereum's network hash rate measures the computational power dedicated to mining and securing the Ethereum blockchain. A higher hash rate indicates a more secure network and greater miner participation, while a lower hash rate may signal potential security vulnerabilities or changes in mining activity.

4. Network Difficulty: Ethereum's network difficulty adjusts dynamically to regulate the rate at which new blocks are mined and maintain a consistent block production time. Changes in network difficulty reflect shifts in mining activity and competition among miners.

5. Total Value Locked (TVL) in DeFi: Total Value Locked (TVL) represents the total value of assets locked in decentralized finance (DeFi) protocols built on the Ethereum blockchain. TVL is a key metric for assessing the adoption and growth of DeFi applications and the overall health of the Ethereum ecosystem.

6. Gas Usage and Fees: Gas usage and fees reflect the level of network activity and congestion on the Ethereum blockchain. Monitor average gas prices, transaction fees, and block sizes to gauge Ethereum's scalability, efficiency, and usability for decentralized applications and transactions.

7. Daily Active Addresses: Daily active addresses measure the number of unique addresses interacting with the Ethereum blockchain on a daily basis. Increasing daily active addresses indicate growing network usage and adoption, while declining active addresses may signal reduced activity or shifting user behavior.

8. Developer Activity: Monitor developer activity on GitHub, Ethereum Improvement Proposals (EIPs), and developer forums to assess the level of innovation, collaboration, and community engagement within the Ethereum ecosystem. High developer activity indicates ongoing protocol improvements and ecosystem growth.

9. Network Upgrades and Protocol Changes: Stay informed about upcoming network upgrades, protocol changes, and Ethereum Improvement Proposals (EIPs) to understand potential impacts on Ethereum's functionality, security, and performance. Follow official Ethereum channels, developer updates, and community discussions to track protocol changes and governance decisions.

Tracking these key metrics and indicators, traders, investors, developers, and stakeholders can gain valuable insights into Ethereum's performance, adoption, and ecosystem dynamics. These metrics provide a comprehensive view of Ethereum's network health, market trends, and fundamental factors driving its long-term value proposition.

CHAPTER 4: DEVELOPING AN INVESTMENT STRATEGY

RISK ASSESSMENT AND MANAGEMENT

Risk assessment and management are essential components of successful cryptocurrency trading and investing, including Ethereum. Here's a guide on how to assess and manage risks associated with Ethereum:

1. Understand the Risks: Familiarize yourself with the risks associated with Ethereum and the cryptocurrency market, including price volatility, regulatory uncertainty, technological risks, security vulnerabilities, liquidity risks, and market manipulation.

2. Conduct Due Diligence: Conduct thorough research and due diligence before investing in Ethereum. Evaluate Ethereum's technology, use cases, adoption, development activity, competition, and regulatory landscape to assess its long-term potential and risks.

3. Determine Risk Tolerance: Determine your risk tolerance based on your investment objectives, financial situation, time horizon, and risk appetite.

Consider factors such as your investment goals, diversification strategy, and willingness to accept short-term volatility and potential losses.

4. Diversify Your Portfolio: Diversify your cryptocurrency portfolio to spread risk across different assets, including Ethereum and other cryptocurrencies, as well as traditional assets such as stocks, bonds, and commodities. Diversification can help reduce portfolio volatility and mitigate the impact of adverse events on individual assets.

5. Set Stop-Loss Orders: Set stop-loss orders to limit potential losses and manage downside risk when trading Ethereum. Determine your risk tolerance and set stop-loss levels based on technical analysis, support levels, and your trading strategy to protect your capital from significant losses during market downturns.

6. Use Position Sizing: Use position sizing techniques to manage risk and allocate capital effectively when trading Ethereum. Determine the appropriate position size based on your risk tolerance, account size, and the level of conviction in your trade setup to avoid overexposure and excessive risk-taking.

7. Implement Risk Management Strategies: Implement risk management strategies, such as dollar-cost averaging, hedging, options trading, and portfolio rebalancing, to mitigate downside risk and preserve capital in volatile market conditions. Adjust your risk management approach based on market conditions, changes in volatility, and evolving risk factors.

8. Stay Informed and Adapt: Stay informed about market developments, news events, and macroeconomic factors that may impact Ethereum's price and risk profile. Continuously monitor market trends, sentiment indicators, and technical analysis signals to adapt your trading and risk management strategies accordingly.

9. Keep Emotions in Check: Keep emotions such as fear, greed, and FOMO (fear of missing out) in check when trading Ethereum. Stick to your trading plan, follow your risk management rules, and avoid making impulsive decisions based on short-term market fluctuations or emotional reactions.

10. Seek Professional Advice: Consider seeking professional advice from financial advisors, investment professionals, or risk management experts to develop a comprehensive risk management strategy tailored to your individual needs and circumstances.

Implementing effective risk assessment and management practices, traders and investors can navigate the complexities of the cryptocurrency market, protect their capital, and improve their chances of achieving long-term success when trading and investing in Ethereum.

DIVERSIFICATION TECHNIQUES

Diversification is a fundamental risk management strategy that involves spreading investments across different assets to reduce exposure to any single asset or risk factor. Here are some diversification techniques you can apply when investing in cryptocurrencies like Ethereum:

1. Asset Diversification: Invest in a diversified portfolio of assets, including Ethereum and other cryptocurrencies, as well as traditional assets such as stocks, bonds, real estate, and commodities. Diversifying across different asset classes can help spread risk and reduce the impact of adverse events on your overall portfolio.

2. Cryptocurrency Diversification: Diversify your cryptocurrency holdings across different cryptocurrencies, tokens, and blockchain projects. Invest in a mix of large-cap, mid-cap, and small-cap cryptocurrencies with varying use cases, development teams, and market dynamics to spread risk and capture opportunities across the cryptocurrency market.

3. Sector Diversification: Diversify your cryptocurrency investments across different sectors and industries within the blockchain ecosystem. Allocate funds to sectors such as decentralized finance (DeFi), non-fungible tokens (NFTs), gaming, supply chain, identity, and interoperability to capitalize on diverse growth opportunities and mitigate sector-specific risks.

4. Geographic Diversification: Consider geographic diversification by investing in cryptocurrencies and blockchain projects based in different countries and regions around the world. Spread risk across different regulatory environments, political landscapes, and economic conditions to reduce exposure to country-specific risks and geopolitical events.

5. Time Diversification: Practice time diversification by dollar-cost averaging (DCA) or investing at regular intervals over time instead of making a lump-sum investment. DCA allows you to average out the cost of your investments and reduce the impact of short-term market volatility on your portfolio.

6. Risk-Based Diversification: Allocate capital based on risk factors such as volatility, liquidity, and correlation coefficients between assets. Adjust your portfolio weighting based on risk levels, with higher allocations to less volatile assets and lower allocations to more volatile assets to achieve a balanced risk-return profile.

7. Portfolio Rebalancing: Periodically rebalance your portfolio to maintain your desired asset allocation and risk profile. Sell assets that have appreciated in value and reallocate funds to underperforming assets to restore your target asset allocation. Rebalancing helps capture gains, manage risk, and align your portfolio with changing market conditions.

8. Stay Informed and Adapt: Stay informed about market developments, emerging trends, and evolving risk factors that may impact your portfolio.

Continuously monitor your investments, assess performance metrics, and adjust your diversification strategy as needed to optimize risk-adjusted returns and achieve your investment goals.

Applying these diversification techniques, you can build a resilient cryptocurrency portfolio that balances risk and return, reduces vulnerability to market fluctuations, and enhances your long-term investment success in the dynamic and evolving cryptocurrency market.

SHORT-TERM VS LONG-TERM INVESTMENT STRATEGIES

Short-term and long-term investment strategies serve different purposes and cater to different investor objectives, risk tolerances, and time horizons. Here's a comparison of short-term and long-term investment strategies:

Short-Term Investment Strategy:
Objective: Short-term investors aim to profit from short-term price movements and capitalize on market volatility. They may seek to generate quick returns, take advantage of trading opportunities, or hedge against short-term risks.

Time Horizon: Short-term investments typically have a time horizon of days, weeks, or months, rather than years. Short-term investors focus on exploiting short-term market trends, news events, and technical indicators to make rapid trades and capture short-term profits.

Risk Tolerance: Short-term investors often have a higher risk tolerance and may be willing to accept higher levels of volatility and uncertainty in exchange for the potential for quick returns. They may engage in margin trading, leverage, and derivatives to amplify gains but also increase the risk of losses.

Strategy: Short-term investment strategies may involve day trading, swing trading, arbitrage, or speculation based on technical analysis, chart patterns, and market sentiment. Short-term investors closely monitor market trends, news catalysts, and price movements to execute timely trades and capitalize on short-term price fluctuations.

Tax Implications: Short-term investments are subject to higher tax rates compared to long-term investments in many jurisdictions. Profits from short-term trades may be taxed as ordinary income, while long-term capital gains may be taxed at lower rates.

Long-Term Investment Strategy:
Objective: Long-term investors focus on building wealth over an extended period by investing in assets with strong fundamentals and growth potential. They prioritize capital preservation, wealth accumulation, and compounding returns over time.

Time Horizon: Long-term investments typically have a time horizon of years, decades, or even generations. Long-term investors take a buy-and-hold approach, allowing investments to appreciate in value over time and benefit from the power of compounding.

Risk Tolerance: Long-term investors tend to have a lower risk tolerance and prioritize stability, diversification, and risk management. They focus on fundamental analysis, asset allocation, and portfolio diversification to mitigate risk and weather market fluctuations over the long term.

Strategy: Long-term investment strategies may involve fundamental analysis, value investing, growth investing, or passive investing through index funds or exchange-traded funds (ETFs). Long-term investors focus on identifying undervalued assets, high-quality companies, and long-term trends with the potential for sustainable growth and long-term value creation.

Tax Implications: Long-term investments are subject to lower tax rates on capital gains compared to short-term investments in many jurisdictions. Profits from long-term investments held for more than a year may qualify for preferential long-term capital gains tax rates.

Short-term and long-term investment strategies each have their advantages and disadvantages, and the most suitable strategy depends on your individual investment goals, risk tolerance, and time horizon. Short-term strategies may offer the potential for quick returns but come with higher risks and tax implications, while long-term strategies prioritize stability, growth, and tax efficiency over time. It's essential to carefully evaluate your investment objectives and choose a strategy that aligns with your financial goals and risk tolerance.

IDENTIFYING ENTRY AND EXIT POINTS

Identifying entry and exit points is crucial for successful trading and investing in cryptocurrencies like Ethereum. Here's how to identify entry and exit points:

1. Technical Analysis:
a. Support and Resistance Levels: Identify key support and resistance levels on Ethereum's price chart using horizontal lines. Support levels represent areas where buying interest may emerge, while resistance levels represent areas where selling pressure may occur. Look for opportunities to enter long positions near support levels and exit near resistance levels.

b. Trendlines: Draw trendlines to identify the direction of the trend and potential trend reversals. An uptrend is characterized by higher highs and higher lows, while a downtrend is characterized by lower highs and lower lows. Look for opportunities to enter long positions in an uptrend and exit near trendline resistance, or enter short positions in a downtrend and exit near trendline support.

c. Moving Averages: Use moving averages, such as the 50-day and 200-day moving averages, to identify trends and potential entry and exit points. In an uptrend, look for opportunities to enter long positions when the price crosses above the moving average (golden cross) and exit when the price crosses below (death cross). In a downtrend, consider short positions when the price is below the moving average and exit when it crosses above.

2. Candlestick Patterns:
a. Reversal Patterns: Look for bullish reversal patterns, such as hammer, bullish engulfing, and morning star, at support levels for potential entry points. Similarly, watch for bearish reversal patterns, such as shooting star, bearish engulfing, and evening star, at resistance levels for potential exit points.

b. Continuation Patterns: Identify continuation patterns, such as flags, pennants, and triangles, within the context of the prevailing trend. Enter positions in the direction of the trend when the price breaks out of the pattern, and consider exiting when the price reaches a predetermined target or shows signs of exhaustion.

3. Volume Analysis:

a. Volume Confirmation: Confirm price movements with volume to validate entry and exit signals. Look for increasing volume during breakouts or trend reversals to confirm the strength of the move. Conversely, be cautious of low volume during consolidations or counter-trend moves, as it may signal weak participation and potential false signals.

4. Market Sentiment:

a. Sentiment Indicators: Monitor market sentiment indicators, such as the Fear and Greed Index, social media sentiment, and sentiment analysis tools, to gauge the overall mood and attitude of market participants. Consider contrarian opportunities when sentiment extremes are reached and align entry and exit points with sentiment trends.

5. Risk Management:

a. Set Stop-Loss Orders: Always set stop-loss orders to limit potential losses and protect your capital. Determine your risk tolerance and set stop-loss levels based on technical analysis, support and resistance levels, and position sizing rules. Adjust stop-loss orders as the trade progresses to lock in profits and minimize downside risk.

b. Take Profit Targets: Define take profit targets based on technical analysis, Fibonacci retracement levels, or price projections. Take profits gradually as the price reaches predetermined targets or shows signs of reversal. Consider trailing stop-loss orders to capture additional gains during strong trends while protecting against potential reversals.

Incorporating these techniques into your trading and investment strategy, you can identify optimal entry and exit points for trading Ethereum and improve your overall profitability and risk-adjusted returns.

CHAPTER 5: ADVANCED INVESTMENT TACTICS

LEVERAGING DECENTRALIZED FINANCE (DEFI)

Leveraging decentralized finance (DeFi) offers various opportunities for earning passive income, accessing financial services, and participating in innovative decentralized applications (dApps) built on blockchain platforms like Ethereum. Here's how you can leverage DeFi:

1. Yield Farming: Participate in yield farming protocols to earn rewards, such as interest, trading fees, or governance tokens, by providing liquidity to decentralized exchanges (DEXs) or liquidity pools. Yield farming involves staking or locking up assets in smart contracts and earning yields in return based on supply and demand dynamics.

2. Liquidity Provision: Provide liquidity to decentralized exchanges (DEXs) like Uniswap, SushiSwap, or Balancer by depositing pairs of assets into liquidity pools. Earn trading fees and additional rewards, such as liquidity mining incentives or governance tokens, based on your share of the liquidity pool.

3. **Staking:** Stake Ethereum or other cryptocurrencies in decentralized staking protocols or networks, such as Ethereum 2.0, to secure the network, validate transactions, and earn staking rewards. Staking involves locking up assets in smart contracts and receiving rewards in return for participating in network consensus.

4. **Lending and Borrowing:** Utilize decentralized lending platforms, such as Compound, Aave, or MakerDAO, to lend out your assets and earn interest or borrow assets against collateralized positions. Earn interest by supplying assets to lending pools or borrow assets for leverage, arbitrage, or short-term trading strategies.

5. **Automated Market Making (AMM):** Participate in automated market making (AMM) protocols, such as Uniswap or Curve Finance, to provide liquidity for decentralized trading pairs and earn trading fees. AMM protocols use algorithms and smart contracts to facilitate peer-to-peer trading without traditional order books.

6. **Decentralized Asset Management:** Explore decentralized asset management platforms, such as Yearn Finance or Harvest Finance, to automate

investment strategies, optimize yield farming opportunities, and maximize returns on your cryptocurrency holdings. These platforms offer yield aggregation, rebalancing, and optimization strategies to enhance portfolio performance.

7. Synthetic Assets: Access synthetic assets and derivatives on decentralized platforms like Synthetix to gain exposure to traditional assets, commodities, or indices without owning the underlying assets. Trade synthetic assets, such as synthetic USD (sUSD) or synthetic Bitcoin (sBTC), to hedge against price fluctuations or speculate on asset prices.

8. Governance Participation: Participate in decentralized autonomous organizations (DAOs) and governance processes to influence decision-making, propose changes, and vote on protocol upgrades or changes. Governance tokens grant holders voting rights and incentives to participate in the governance of decentralized protocols.

9. Risk Management: Assess the risks associated with DeFi protocols, including smart contract vulnerabilities, impermanent loss, collateralization ratios, liquidation risks, and market volatility.

Conduct due diligence, diversify your investments, and implement risk management strategies to mitigate potential risks and protect your assets.

By leveraging DeFi protocols and platforms, you can access a wide range of financial services, earn passive income, and participate in decentralized applications and governance processes while maintaining control over your assets and interacting directly with blockchain networks without intermediaries. However, it's essential to conduct thorough research, understand the risks involved, and exercise caution when participating in DeFi activities.

YIELD FARMING AND STAKING

Yield farming and staking are two popular DeFi strategies for earning passive income and participating in blockchain networks like Ethereum. Here's how they work:

1. Yield Farming:

Definition: Yield farming, also known as liquidity mining, involves providing liquidity to decentralized finance (DeFi) protocols by locking up assets in liquidity pools or yield farming strategies to earn rewards, such as interest, trading fees, or governance tokens.

How it Works:
a. Choose a DeFi protocol: Select a decentralized lending, borrowing, or decentralized exchange (DEX) platform that offers yield farming opportunities, such as Compound, Aave, Uniswap, or SushiSwap.
b. Provide liquidity: Deposit pairs of assets into liquidity pools or yield farming strategies, such as ETH/DAI or ETH/USDC, to supply liquidity to the protocol and earn rewards.
c. Earn rewards: Earn rewards in the form of interest, trading fees, or governance tokens based on your share of the liquidity pool and the volume of transactions processed by the protocol.

d. Manage your positions: Monitor your yield farming positions, adjust your asset allocations, and compound your earnings over time to maximize returns and optimize your yield farming strategy.

Benefits:
- **Potential for high yields:** Yield farming offers the potential for high yields compared to traditional savings accounts or fixed-income investments.
- **Access to DeFi protocols:** Participate in decentralized finance (DeFi) protocols, earn rewards, and contribute to the growth of the DeFi ecosystem.
- **Diversification:** Diversify your cryptocurrency holdings and earn passive income by providing liquidity to multiple DeFi protocols and liquidity pools.

Risks:
- **Impermanent loss:** Risk of impermanent loss due to fluctuations in asset prices and changes in liquidity pool ratios.
- **Smart contract risks:** Vulnerability to smart contract bugs, exploits, or security breaches in DeFi protocols.
- **Market volatility:** Exposure to market volatility and price fluctuations of underlying assets in liquidity pools.

- **Protocol risks:** Risks associated with the governance, security, and sustainability of DeFi protocols and platforms.

2. Staking:

Definition: Staking involves locking up cryptocurrencies in a staking wallet or smart contract to participate in the consensus mechanism of a blockchain network, validate transactions, and earn staking rewards.

How it Works:
a. Choose a staking network: Select a blockchain network that supports staking, such as Ethereum 2.0, Polkadot, Cardano, or Cosmos.
b. Stake your assets: Lock up a certain amount of cryptocurrencies, such as ETH, DOT, ADA, or ATOM, in a staking wallet or smart contract to participate in network consensus.
c. Validate transactions: Support the network by validating transactions, processing blocks, and securing the blockchain in exchange for staking rewards.
d. Earn rewards: Earn staking rewards in the form of additional cryptocurrency tokens, such as ETH2, DOT, ADA, or ATOM, based on your staked balance and contribution to network security.

Benefits:
- **Passive income:** Earn passive income by staking cryptocurrencies and participating in the consensus mechanism of blockchain networks.
- **Network participation:** Contribute to the security, decentralization, and scalability of blockchain networks by staking your assets and validating transactions.
- **Long-term investment:** Stake cryptocurrencies for the long term to earn staking rewards and potentially benefit from price appreciation over time.

Risks:
- **Slashing risks:** Risk of losing a portion of your staked assets as a penalty for malicious behavior or protocol violations, such as double-signing or downtime.
- **Lock-up period:** Inability to access staked assets during the lock-up period, which may vary depending on the staking protocol and network.
- **Network risks:** Risks associated with the security, scalability, and governance of blockchain networks and staking protocols.

Yield farming and staking offer attractive opportunities for earning passive income, participating in DeFi protocols, and contributing to the growth of blockchain networks. However, it's essential to understand the risks involved, conduct thorough research, and carefully assess the potential returns and rewards before engaging in yield farming or staking activities. By diversifying your strategies, managing your risks, and staying informed about market developments, you can leverage yield farming and staking to optimize your returns and achieve your financial goals in the dynamic and evolving cryptocurrency landscape.

UTILIZING ETHEREUM DERIVATIVES

Utilizing Ethereum derivatives involves trading financial instruments whose value is derived from the price of Ethereum (ETH). Derivatives allow investors to speculate on Ethereum's price movements, hedge against price volatility, and manage risk exposure. Here are some common Ethereum derivatives and how they can be utilized:

1. Futures Contracts:

Definition: Futures contracts are agreements to buy or sell Ethereum at a predetermined price (the futures price) on a specified future date. They enable investors to speculate on Ethereum's future price movements without owning the underlying asset.

How to Utilize:
a. Speculative trading: Take long or short positions in Ethereum futures contracts based on your market outlook and trading strategy. Profit from price movements by buying (going long) or selling (going short) futures contracts.
b. Hedging: Hedge against price risk by taking opposite positions in Ethereum futures contracts to offset potential losses or lock in profits from spot positions.

2. Options Contracts:

Definition: Options contracts give the holder the right, but not the obligation, to buy (call option) or sell (put option) Ethereum at a predetermined price (the strike price) on or before a specified expiration date. They offer flexibility and leverage for traders and investors.

How to Utilize:
a. Speculative trading: Buy call options to profit from Ethereum's price appreciation or buy put options to profit from price declines. Sell call options or put options to earn premiums and generate income.
b. Hedging: Hedge against downside risk by buying put options as insurance against price

declines. Write covered call options against existing Ethereum holdings to generate additional income.

3. Perpetual Swaps:
Definition: Perpetual swaps are derivative contracts that mimic the features of futures contracts but have no expiration date. They allow investors to trade Ethereum with leverage and without the need for margin funding or rolling over positions.

How to Utilize:
a. Leverage trading: Trade Ethereum with leverage by entering long or short positions in perpetual swaps. Utilize leverage to amplify potential returns, but be aware of increased risk and potential liquidation.
b. Arbitrage opportunities: Exploit price discrepancies between Ethereum spot markets and perpetual swap markets to profit from arbitrage opportunities.

4. Exchange-Traded Funds (ETFs) and Exchange-Traded Products (ETPs):
Definition: ETFs and ETPs are investment products that track the price of Ethereum or Ethereum-related indices. They allow investors to

gain exposure to Ethereum without directly holding the underlying asset.

How to Utilize:
a. Diversification: Invest in Ethereum ETFs or ETPs to gain exposure to Ethereum and diversify your portfolio across different assets and asset classes.
b. Risk management: Use Ethereum ETFs or ETPs as a risk management tool to hedge against specific risks or sectors in your investment portfolio.

5. Margin Trading:
Definition: Margin trading allows investors to borrow funds from a broker or exchange to trade Ethereum with leverage. It amplifies both potential profits and losses and requires maintaining a margin balance to cover losses.

How to Utilize:
a. Leverage trading: Trade Ethereum with leverage by borrowing funds to increase your trading capital. Use leverage to amplify potential returns, but be cautious of increased risk and potential margin calls.
b. Risk management: Manage risk exposure by setting stop-loss orders, maintaining adequate

margin levels, and avoiding excessive leverage when margin trading Ethereum.

Utilizing Ethereum derivatives offers opportunities for speculation, hedging, leverage trading, and risk management in the cryptocurrency market. However, derivatives trading involves inherent risks, including price volatility, leverage risk, counterparty risk, and liquidity risk. It's essential to conduct thorough research, understand the mechanics of derivatives products, and use risk management strategies to protect your capital and achieve your investment objectives when trading Ethereum derivatives.

NAVIGATING MARKET VOLATILITY

Navigating market volatility is essential for successfully trading and investing in Ethereum and other cryptocurrencies. Here are some strategies to help you navigate market volatility effectively:

1. Risk Management:

a. Position Sizing: Determine the appropriate size for each trade based on your risk tolerance, account size, and the level of confidence in your trading strategy. Avoid risking more than a small percentage of your trading capital on any single trade to minimize potential losses.

b. Stop-Loss Orders: Set stop-loss orders to limit potential losses and protect your capital from significant downturns. Place stop-loss orders at strategic levels based on technical analysis, support and resistance levels, and your risk management rules.

c. Diversification: Diversify your cryptocurrency portfolio across different assets, sectors, and strategies to spread risk and reduce vulnerability to individual market movements. Consider allocating funds to a mix of cryptocurrencies, stablecoins, and traditional assets to hedge against volatility.

2. Technical Analysis:

a. Support and Resistance Levels: Identify key support and resistance levels on Ethereum's price chart to anticipate potential reversals or breakouts. Support levels represent areas where buying interest may emerge, while resistance levels represent areas where selling pressure may occur.

b. Trend Analysis: Analyze the direction and strength of the trend using trendlines, moving averages, and chart patterns. Follow the trend and look for opportunities to enter long positions in uptrends or short positions in downtrends to align with the prevailing market direction.

c. Volatility Indicators: Use volatility indicators, such as Bollinger Bands, Average True Range (ATR), or the Volatility Index (VIX), to measure market volatility and identify potential trading opportunities. High volatility may present opportunities for profit, but also increases the risk of losses.

3. Fundamental Analysis:

a. News and Events: Stay informed about market-moving news, events, and developments that may impact Ethereum's price and market sentiment. Monitor regulatory announcements, technological advancements, partnerships, and adoption trends to anticipate market movements.

b. Network Fundamentals: Evaluate Ethereum's network fundamentals, including transaction volume, network activity, developer activity, and adoption metrics, to gauge the underlying strength and value of the Ethereum ecosystem.

4. Emotion Control:

a. Stay Calm: Keep emotions such as fear, greed, and panic in check when trading and investing in volatile markets. Stick to your trading plan, follow your risk management rules, and avoid making impulsive decisions based on short-term price movements.

b. Maintain Discipline: Stick to your trading strategy, regardless of market conditions, and avoid chasing quick gains or trying to time the market. Maintain discipline, patience, and consistency in your approach to trading and investing in Ethereum.

5. Continuous Learning:

a. Stay Educated: Continuously educate yourself about trading strategies, technical analysis techniques, and market dynamics to improve your trading skills and adapt to changing market conditions.

b. Learn from Mistakes: Review your trading performance, analyze past trades, and learn from your mistakes to refine your strategy, improve decision-making, and avoid repeating costly errors.

Implementing these strategies and techniques, you can navigate market volatility more effectively, minimize risks, and increase your chances of success when trading and investing in Ethereum and other cryptocurrencies.

CHAPTER 6: MONITORING AND ADJUSTING YOUR PORTFOLIO

PERFORMANCE TRACKING TOOLS

Performance tracking tools are essential for monitoring and evaluating the performance of your investments in Ethereum and other cryptocurrencies. Here are some popular tools and platforms for tracking the performance of your crypto portfolio:

1. CoinMarketCap: CoinMarketCap is one of the most widely used cryptocurrency tracking websites that provides real-time data on cryptocurrency prices, market capitalization, trading volume, and price charts for thousands of cryptocurrencies, including Ethereum. You can create a watchlist of your favorite cryptocurrencies and track their performance over time.

2. CoinGecko: CoinGecko is another popular cryptocurrency data aggregator that offers comprehensive information on cryptocurrency prices, market capitalization, trading volume, and historical data. It also provides additional metrics such as developer activity, community engagement, and liquidity to help you assess the overall health and performance of cryptocurrencies like Ethereum.

3. Blockfolio: Blockfolio is a mobile app that allows you to track the performance of your cryptocurrency portfolio in real-time. You can add your Ethereum holdings and other cryptocurrencies, track their prices, set price alerts, and view your portfolio's overall performance over time. Blockfolio also offers news and updates from the cryptocurrency market.

4. Delta: Delta is another popular cryptocurrency portfolio tracker app available on both mobile and desktop platforms. It provides real-time price updates, portfolio tracking, and customizable alerts for your Ethereum holdings and other cryptocurrencies. Delta offers a user-friendly interface and supports multiple fiat currencies and exchanges.

5. CryptoCompare: CryptoCompare offers a wide range of cryptocurrency data and tools, including real-time prices, historical data, news, and portfolio tracking. You can create a personalized cryptocurrency portfolio, track your Ethereum investments, and analyze performance metrics using CryptoCompare's comprehensive dashboard.

6. CoinStats: CoinStats is a cryptocurrency portfolio tracker app that offers real-time price updates, portfolio management tools, and performance analytics. You can sync your Ethereum holdings and other cryptocurrencies across multiple devices, set price alerts, and view detailed charts and statistics to monitor your portfolio's performance.

7. TradingView: TradingView is a popular charting platform that allows you to analyze cryptocurrency prices, technical indicators, and trading patterns. You can create custom watchlists, set price alerts, and access a wide range of charting tools and indicators to track the performance of Ethereum and other cryptocurrencies.

8. Excel or Google Sheets: For more advanced users, creating a custom portfolio tracker using Excel or Google Sheets allows for flexibility and customization. You can import data from cryptocurrency exchanges or use APIs to fetch real-time prices, calculate portfolio performance metrics, and create custom dashboards to monitor your Ethereum investments.

By using these performance tracking tools and platforms, you can stay informed about the performance of your Ethereum investments, track market trends, and make informed decisions to optimize your portfolio's performance in the dynamic and evolving cryptocurrency market.

REBALANCING YOUR PORTFOLIO

Rebalancing your portfolio is essential for maintaining an optimal asset allocation, managing risk, and maximizing returns over time. Here's a guide on how to rebalance your cryptocurrency portfolio, including Ethereum:

1. Establish a Rebalancing Strategy:

a. Frequency: Determine how often you will rebalance your portfolio based on market conditions, your investment goals, and your risk tolerance. Common rebalancing frequencies include quarterly, semi-annually, or annually.

b. Thresholds: Set target allocation percentages for each asset in your portfolio, including Ethereum, and establish rebalancing thresholds to trigger portfolio adjustments. Rebalance your portfolio when asset allocations deviate significantly from the target percentages.

c. Method: Decide on a rebalancing method, such as strategic or tactical rebalancing. Strategic rebalancing involves periodically realigning your portfolio back to its target allocations, while tactical rebalancing involves making adjustments based on market conditions or changes in investment outlook.

2. Assess Portfolio Performance:

a. Review Asset Performance: Evaluate the performance of each asset in your portfolio, including Ethereum, relative to its target allocation and benchmark indices. Identify assets that have outperformed or underperformed and assess their contribution to portfolio returns.

b. Analyze Market Trends: Monitor market trends, macroeconomic factors, and industry developments that may impact the performance of your portfolio assets, including Ethereum. Consider adjusting your portfolio allocations based on changing market conditions and emerging opportunities.

3. Determine Rebalancing Actions:

a. Buy or Sell Assets: Determine whether to buy or sell assets in your portfolio to realign your allocations with the target percentages. If Ethereum's weight has increased relative to other assets, consider selling a portion of your Ethereum holdings and reinvesting the proceeds into underweight assets. Conversely, if Ethereum's weight has decreased, consider buying more Ethereum to maintain the target allocation.

b. Tax Considerations: Consider the tax implications of rebalancing your portfolio, especially when selling assets with capital gains. Utilize tax-efficient strategies, such as tax-loss harvesting or using tax-advantaged accounts, to minimize the impact of taxes on portfolio returns.

4. Execute Rebalancing Trades:

a. Place Orders: Execute rebalancing trades by placing buy or sell orders on cryptocurrency exchanges or trading platforms. Use limit orders to specify the desired price for executing trades and avoid market slippage.

b. Monitor Execution: Monitor the execution of rebalancing trades and ensure that transactions are completed accurately and in a timely manner.

Verify that portfolio allocations have been adjusted according to the rebalancing plan.

5. Review and Adjust:

a. Monitor Performance: Continuously monitor the performance of your rebalanced portfolio and track the impact of portfolio adjustments on returns, risk, and asset allocations. Evaluate whether the rebalancing strategy is achieving the desired outcomes and make adjustments as necessary.

b. Reassess Strategy: Periodically reassess your rebalancing strategy and make adjustments based on changes in market conditions, investment objectives, or risk tolerance. Consider refinements to your target allocations, rebalancing thresholds, or rebalancing frequency to optimize portfolio performance over time.

Following these steps and implementing a disciplined rebalancing strategy, you can maintain a well-diversified and optimized cryptocurrency portfolio, manage risk effectively, and maximize returns over the long term, including your investments in Ethereum.

ADAPTING TO MARKET CHANGES

Adapting to market changes is crucial for successfully navigating the dynamic and unpredictable cryptocurrency landscape. Here are some strategies to help you adapt to market changes effectively, including those affecting Ethereum:

1. Stay Informed:

a. Market Analysis: Continuously monitor market trends, news, and developments that may impact the price and performance of Ethereum and other cryptocurrencies. Stay informed about regulatory updates, technological advancements, adoption trends, and macroeconomic factors affecting the cryptocurrency market.

b. Research: Conduct thorough research on Ethereum's fundamentals, including its technology, network upgrades, developer activity, and ecosystem developments. Stay updated on Ethereum Improvement Proposals (EIPs), protocol changes, and community initiatives to assess the long-term prospects of Ethereum.

2. Adapt Your Strategy:

a. Flexibility: Be flexible and adaptable in your trading and investment strategy to respond to changing market conditions and emerging opportunities. Adjust your approach based on evolving trends, market dynamics, and your risk tolerance.

b. Diversification: Diversify your cryptocurrency portfolio across different assets, sectors, and strategies to mitigate risk and capitalize on diverse growth opportunities. Allocate funds to a mix of cryptocurrencies, stablecoins, and traditional assets to hedge against volatility and market uncertainty.

3. Risk Management:

a. Position Sizing: Manage risk by determining the appropriate size for each trade or investment based on your risk tolerance, account size, and the level of conviction in your analysis. Avoid overexposure to any single asset or position to minimize potential losses.

b. Stop-Loss Orders: Use stop-loss orders to limit downside risk and protect your capital from significant losses during market downturns. Set stop-loss levels based on technical analysis, support and resistance levels, and your risk management rules.

4. Monitor Performance:

a. Portfolio Review: Regularly review the performance of your cryptocurrency portfolio, including your investments in Ethereum. Assess the impact of market changes on portfolio returns, risk exposure, and asset allocations.

b. Performance Analysis: Analyze the performance of individual assets, trading strategies, and investment decisions to identify strengths, weaknesses, and areas for improvement. Learn from past experiences and adjust your approach accordingly to optimize future performance.

5. Stay Patient and Disciplined:

a. Patience: Practice patience and avoid making impulsive decisions based on short-term market fluctuations or emotional reactions. Stick to your trading plan, investment thesis, and risk management rules, even during periods of market volatility.

b. Discipline: Maintain discipline in your trading and investment approach, regardless of market conditions or external factors. Follow your strategy consistently, execute trades with discipline, and avoid deviating from your plan due to fear, greed, or FOMO (fear of missing out).

6. Continuous Learning:

a. Education: Continuously educate yourself about cryptocurrency markets, trading strategies, technical analysis techniques, and risk management principles. Stay updated on industry trends, best practices, and lessons learned from experienced traders and investors.

b. Adaptation: Adapt and evolve your skills, knowledge, and strategies over time to keep pace with the changing dynamics of the cryptocurrency market. Embrace new technologies, tools, and methodologies that can enhance your trading and investment capabilities.

Implementing these strategies and principles, you can adapt to market changes effectively, mitigate risks, and capitalize on opportunities to achieve your trading and investment goals in the dynamic and evolving cryptocurrency landscape, including your investments in Ethereum.

LEARNING FROM INVESTMENT MISTAKES

Learning from investment mistakes is essential for improving your trading and investing skills and avoiding costly errors in the future. Here's how you can learn from your investment mistakes, including those related to Ethereum:

1. Reflect on Your Decisions:

a. Analyze the Trade: Review the details of the investment or trade, including the rationale behind your decision, the timing of the trade, and the factors influencing your choice to buy or sell Ethereum.

b. Identify Mistakes: Identify any mistakes or errors in judgment that may have contributed to the outcome of the trade. Consider whether you overlooked important information, misinterpreted market signals, or failed to adhere to your trading plan or risk management rules.

2. Understand the Root Causes:

a. Emotional Biases: Recognize and address emotional biases, such as fear, greed, overconfidence, or FOMO (fear of missing out), that may have influenced your decision-making process.

Avoid making impulsive decisions based on emotions and strive to maintain objectivity in your analysis.

b. Lack of Research: Acknowledge any gaps in your research or analysis that may have led to uninformed decisions. Commit to conducting thorough research, performing due diligence, and staying informed about market developments before making investment decisions.

3. Adjust Your Approach:

a. Update Your Strategy: Update your trading or investment strategy based on lessons learned from past mistakes. Adjust your approach, refine your criteria for entering or exiting trades, and incorporate risk management techniques to minimize future losses.

b. Set Realistic Expectations: Set realistic expectations for your investments and avoid chasing unrealistic returns or trying to time the market. Focus on consistent, disciplined trading and investment practices, rather than seeking quick profits or speculating on short-term price movements.

4. Implement Risk Management:

a. Position Sizing: Implement proper position sizing techniques to manage risk and avoid overexposure to any single asset or position. Determine the appropriate size for each trade based on your risk tolerance, account size, and the level of conviction in your analysis.

b. Use Stop-Loss Orders: Utilize stop-loss orders to limit potential losses and protect your capital from significant downturns. Set stop-loss levels based on technical analysis, support and resistance levels, and your risk management rules.

5. Continuous Improvement:

a. Learn from Others: Seek feedback and advice from experienced traders, investors, or mentors who can offer valuable insights and perspectives on your investment approach. Learn from their experiences, strategies, and mistakes to improve your skills and knowledge.

b. Practice Discipline: Maintain discipline in your trading and investment approach, even in the face of market volatility or external pressures. Stick to your trading plan, follow your risk management rules, and avoid deviating from your strategy based on emotions or short-term market fluctuations.

6. Keep Records:

a. Track Your Performance: Keep detailed records of your trades, investments, and portfolio performance to track your progress over time. Analyze your performance metrics, review your trading journal, and identify patterns or trends that may impact your investment decisions.

b. Review Regularly: Regularly review your trading journal, analyze past trades, and reflect on your performance to identify areas for improvement and make adjustments to your strategy accordingly.

By learning from your investment mistakes, analyzing your decisions, and adjusting your approach, you can become a more disciplined, knowledgeable, and successful trader or investor in Ethereum and other cryptocurrencies over time.

CONCLUSION

Investing in Ethereum and navigating the cryptocurrency market requires careful planning, disciplined execution, and continuous learning. Ethereum, with its innovative technology, decentralized applications, and growing ecosystem, offers unique opportunities for investors and traders alike. However, it's essential to approach Ethereum investment with caution and diligence, considering the inherent risks and market volatility associated with cryptocurrencies.

By understanding Ethereum's fundamentals, staying informed about market trends, and utilizing effective trading and investment strategies, you can capitalize on opportunities, manage risk, and optimize your returns over time. Whether you're a long-term investor or a short-term trader, adapting to market changes, learning from investment mistakes, and maintaining discipline are key to achieving success in the dynamic and evolving cryptocurrency landscape.

As you embark on your journey in Ethereum investment, remember to set realistic goals, diversify your portfolio, and implement risk management techniques to protect your capital and achieve your financial objectives. Stay patient, stay informed, and stay adaptable to market conditions, and you'll be well-positioned to navigate the challenges and opportunities that Ethereum and the cryptocurrency market present.

Above all, remember that investing in Ethereum and cryptocurrencies carries inherent risks, and past performance is not indicative of future results. Exercise caution, conduct thorough research, and seek advice from qualified professionals when needed. With a balanced approach and a commitment to continuous improvement, you can navigate the exciting world of Ethereum investment with confidence and resilience.

www.ingramcontent.com/pod-product-compliance
Lightning Source LLC
Chambersburg PA
CBHW070115230526
45472CB00004B/1274